THE NATURE KIDS GUIDE TO
ZEBRAS

DAVID ANDERSON

LP Media Inc. Publishing
Text copyright © 2026 by LP Media Inc.
All rights reserved.

For information address LP Media Inc. Publishing,
30012 Variolite St NW, Princeton MN 55371
www.lpmedia.org

Publication Data

Zebras
The Nature Kid's Guide to Zebras — First edition.

Summary: "Learn all about Zebras, the Nature Kid Way"
— Provided by publisher.

ISBN: 979-8-89818-116-1

[1. Zebras – Non-Fiction] I. Title.

Title: The Nature Kid's Guide to Zebras

CONTENTS

GRASSY GROUND

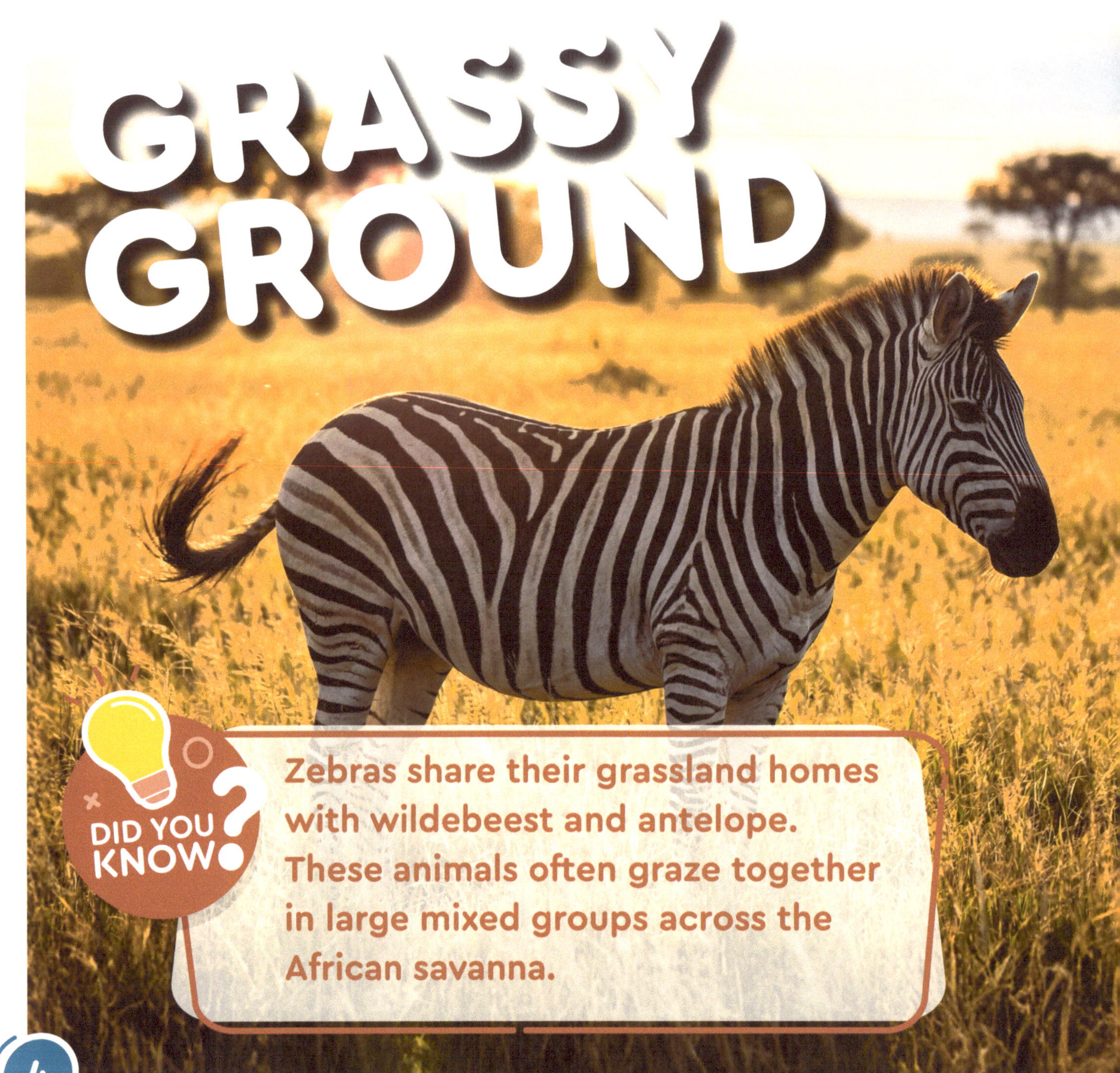

Zebras share their grassland homes with wildebeest and antelope. These animals often graze together in large mixed groups across the African savanna.

Neigh! A zebra stands in tall grass. Its black and white stripes shine.

Zebras roam across wide grasslands called **savannas**. These open spaces have lots of tall grass and few trees. The air feels warm and dry.

Zebras need grass to eat and water to drink. Fresh water holes dot the land. Some zebras live in dry areas with short, golden grass.

Other zebras live near mountains. These places have green valleys and rocky slopes. The air is cooler there.

All zebras need open land. They must see far to spot danger. Grasslands give them room to run fast and stay safe.

AFRICAN ADVENTURES

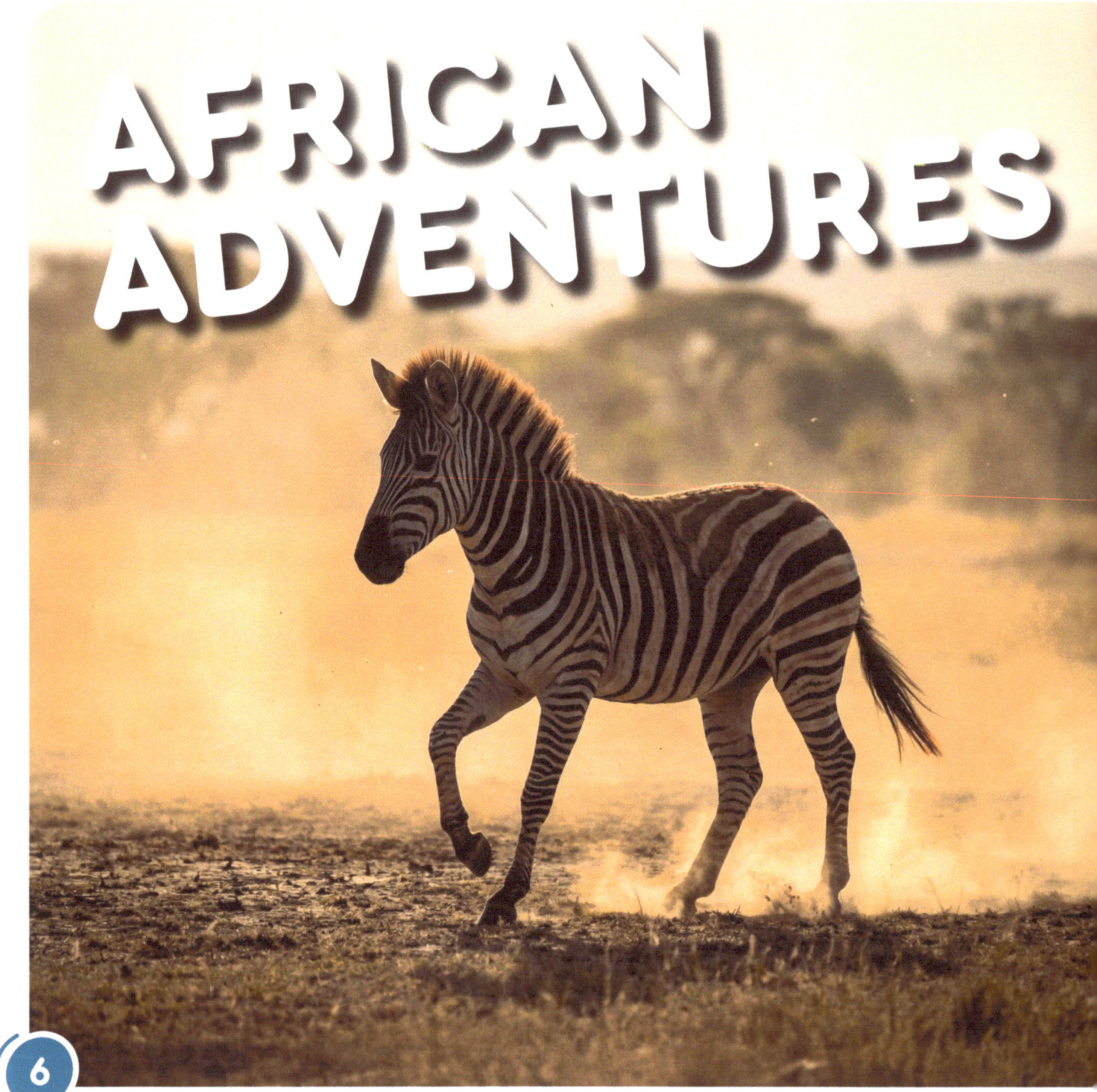

Thump! A zebra trots across dry land, kicking up dust.

Zebras live only in Africa. You will not find them anywhere else in the wild!

Plains zebras roam East Africa. They live in Kenya and Tanzania. They travel the **Serengeti** plains.

Mountain zebras stay in southern Africa. They live in Namibia and South Africa.

Grevy's zebras have a small home. They live only in Ethiopia and northern Kenya.

Grevy's zebras are the largest wild horse type. They can weigh up to 990 pounds!

SIZING UP

Stomp! A big zebra walks next to a small one. They look so different!

Zebras come in different sizes. Plains zebras are medium sized. They weigh about 770 pounds, which is as heavy as four adult humans!

Grevy's zebras are the biggest. They can weigh up to 990 pounds and stand taller than other zebras too.

Mountain zebras are smaller. They weigh around 600 pounds. No matter their size, all zebras have strong bodies built for running fast.

Baby zebras are born with legs almost as long as an adult's. They can stand up in just 15 minutes and run within one hour!

SUPER STRIPES

A zebra's skin under its fur is black. The white stripes are just in the hair!

Swoosh! A zebra swishes its striped tail in the sun.

Every zebra has stripes, but no two zebras look exactly the same. Their stripe patterns are unique, like human fingerprints.

Stripes cover most of the body. They wrap around the legs and belly, though some zebras have white bellies. Even the mane has stripes that stand up straight.

The three types of zebras have different stripe patterns. Plains zebras have wide stripes. Grevy's zebras have thin stripes close together. Mountain zebras have a grid pattern of stripes on their rumps.

12

Snort! A zebra lifts its head. Its ears twist around.

Zebras have excellent senses. Their eyes sit on the sides of their head. This helps them see almost all around.

Zebra ears can turn in different directions. Each ear moves on its own to listen for lions and other predators.

Zebras also have a strong sense of smell. They can find water far away.

Zebras can see in color and also see well at night, even in dim light.

STRIPE SHIELD

Buzz! Flies swarm near a zebra. But then they fly away fast.

Zebra stripes may confuse biting flies. Scientists think the pattern makes it hard for flies to land. This helps keep zebras healthy.

Stripes might also confuse predators. When zebras run together, all the stripes blur. This makes it hard to pick out just one zebra.

Scientists are still testing if stripes help zebras stay cool. Dark stripes get hotter than white stripes.

Some airports paint zebra-like stripes on runways to keep birds away from planes.

15

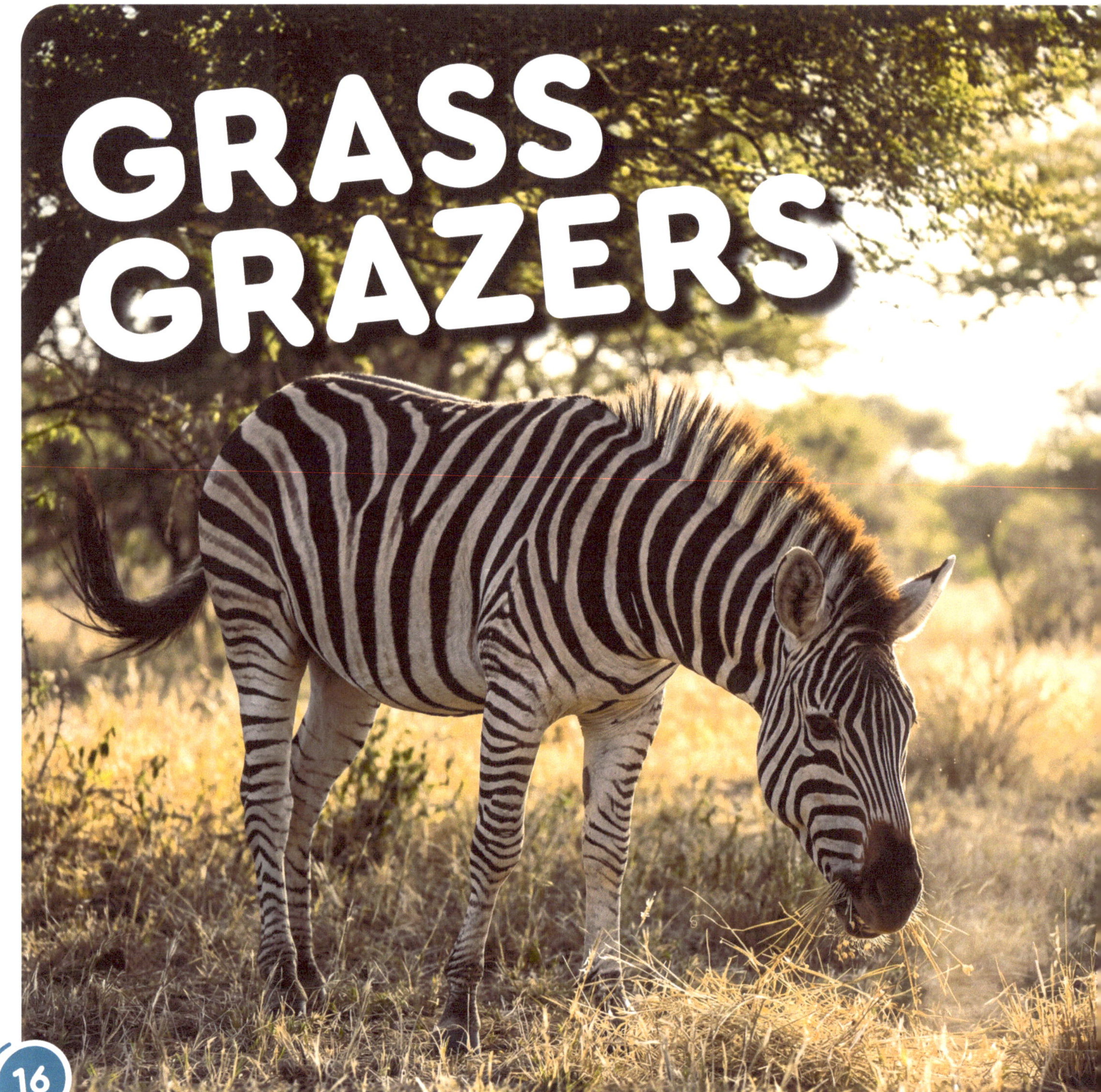

GRASS
GRAZERS
16

Crunch! A zebra bites off a mouthful of dry grass.

Zebras eat grass. They spend most of their day grazing, using their strong teeth to cut through tough grass stems.

Zebras can eat grass that other animals cannot. They digest old, dry grass well, which helps them survive when food is hard to find.

Zebras also need lots of water. They drink every day when water is nearby. During dry times, they travel far to find rivers and water holes.

Zebras can eat grass for up to 18 hours a day.

ZEBRA SIGNALS

A zebra's bray can be heard from over a mile away on the open plains.

Snort! A zebra lifts its head. It hears a sound.

Zebras make many sounds. They bark, snort, and bray. Each sound has a meaning. A loud bark warns of danger. A soft nicker greets a friend.

Zebras also use body language. They point their ears forward when alert. Flat ears show anger. A zebra may stomp its hoof to get attention.

Foals call to their mothers with high squeals. Mothers answer with soft sounds. This helps them find each other in a big herd.

Zebras stay safe by talking to each other.

DANGER ZONE

Growl! A lion crouches in the grass. A zebra looks up fast.

Zebras face many predators. Lions hunt them. Hyenas hunt them. Wild dogs hunt them too. Cheetahs and leopards also attack zebras.

Lions are the main threat. These big cats usually hunt at night. Zebras must stay alert.

Young zebras are in more danger. They cannot run as fast. Predators often go after foals first.

This is why groups help. Zebras spot danger fast together.

Crocodiles can grab zebras when they cross rivers during migration season.

KICK BACK
22

Crack! A zebra kicks its back legs high in the air.

Zebras have strong legs. They use them to run fast and to fight back against predators.

A zebra's kick is very powerful. One kick can hurt a lion badly. This makes predators try to avoid a zebra's kicking legs.

Zebras also bite when in danger. Their teeth are sharp and strong. A zebra fights hard to stay safe.

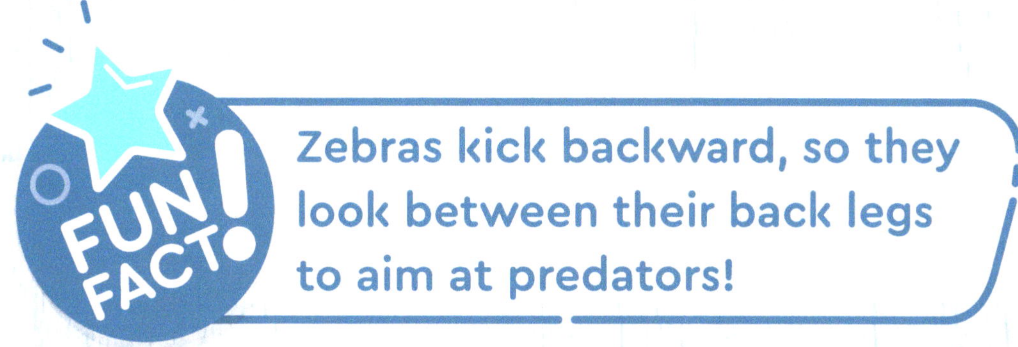

ZOOM ZOOM

Whoosh! A zebra races across the plain. Dust flies behind it.

Zebras run fast. They can go 40 miles per hour. This helps them stay safe. In Africa only cheetahs, lions, and wild dogs can run faster.

Zebras run in a zigzag path. This makes it hard for hunters to catch them.

Zebras can also run for a long time without getting tired. They travel many miles to find fresh grass and water. Some herds walk over 1,000 miles each year looking for food.

A zebra foal can run with the herd just one hour after being born to escape predators.

DAILY LIFE

Rustle! A zebra wakes at dawn and stretches its legs.

Zebras are active during the day. They spend most of their time eating and walking. The herd moves slowly across the grassland.

During the hottest part of the day, zebras rest in the shade. They stand close together to stay cool. Some zebras sleep while others watch for danger.

Zebras groom each other too. They nibble on each other's coats to stay clean.

Zebras take short naps that last only about seven minutes. They must stay alert for danger.

DAZZLING
HERDS
28

Grunt! A zebra calls out. The whole herd looks up.

Zebras live in groups. These groups are called herds. A herd can have many zebras. They stay together to be safe.

Baby zebras learn their mother's stripes. Since each zebra has its own pattern, they can find their mother even in a large crowd.

Herds often walk with wildebeest. They walk with antelope too. More eyes can watch for danger this way.

A group of zebras is sometimes called a dazzle because their stripes look dazzling together.

FINDING LOVE

Rub! Two zebras touch noses and sniff each other.

Zebras can mate any time of year. Most foals are born in the rainy season. The grass is green then. There is lots of food.

Male zebras are called stallions. Female zebras are called mares. A stallion leads a small family group.

Mares have one foal at a time. A mare is pregnant for twelve months. Then the foal is born.

Zebra stallions will fight other males by biting and kicking to protect their family group.

FUZZY FOALS

32

Cute! A baby zebra stands on wobbly legs. It takes its very first steps.

A baby zebra is called a foal. Foals are born with brown and white stripes. Their stripes turn black as they grow older.

Newborn foals can stand within minutes. They can run within an hour. They have to be able to run quickly in case predators come near.

Foals drink milk from their mothers. They start eating grass after a few weeks. A foal stays close to its mother for the first year. Their fuzzy coats keep them warm during the cool African nights.

GROWING UP

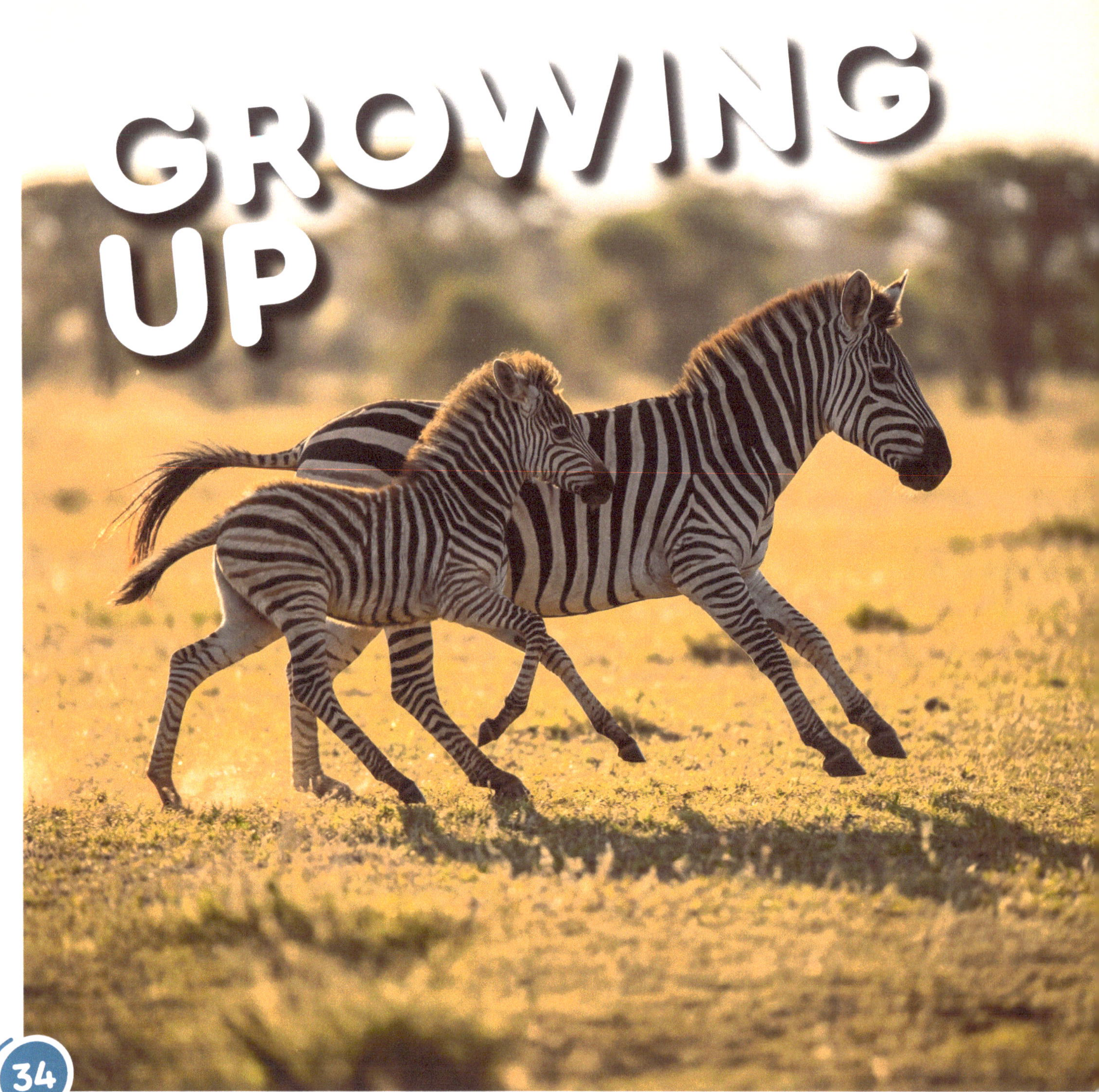

Thump! A young zebra runs beside its mother across the grassy plain.

Young zebras grow up fast. They learn by watching older zebras. They copy how adults eat, drink, and stay safe.

Foals play with other young zebras in the herd. They chase and nip at each other. Playing helps them build strong muscles.

A young zebra stays with its mother for one to three years. Then it joins other zebras its age. Male zebras then leave to form **bachelor** groups.

Young zebras recognize their mother by her stripes, scent, and voice.

SHRINKING LAND

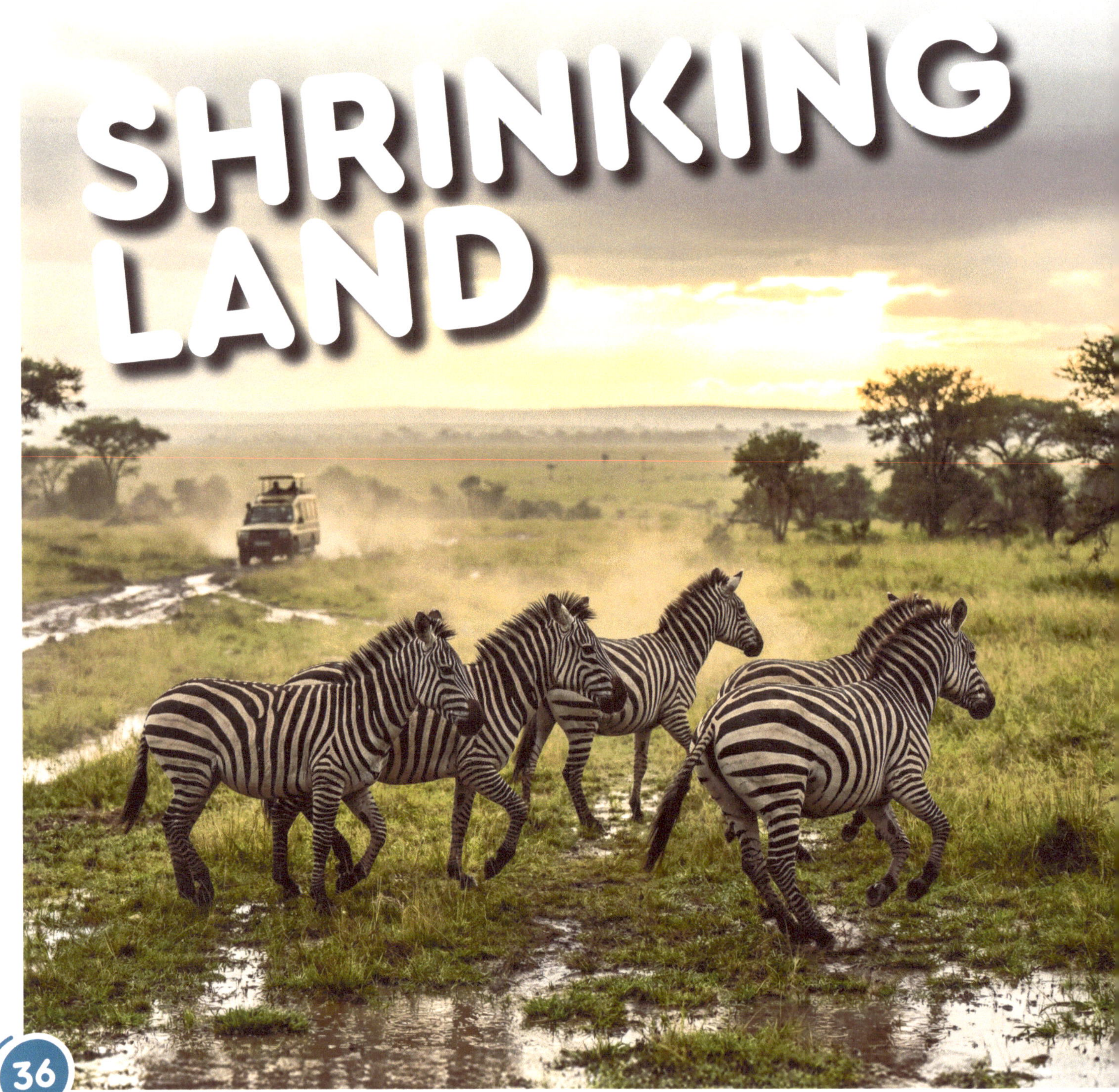

Rumble! A truck drives near zebras. The loud noise scares them away.

Zebras face many dangers today. People build farms and roads on zebra land. This leaves less space for zebras to roam.

Some people hunt zebras for their skins. This is called **poaching**, and it is against the law.

Droughts make water hard to find. Zebras must travel farther to survive.

Grevy's zebras are endangered. Only about 3,000 live in the wild today. They are the largest wild horse species.

SAVING STRIPES

Click! A camera snaps a photo. Rangers use these to watch zebras.

People work to save zebras. Rangers guard them. They stop poachers. They watch parks day and night.

Scientists study zebra herds. They count the zebras. They also track where zebras travel. This helps them know if zebra numbers are going up or down.

New parks give zebras more land. Many groups around the world raise money to protect zebras and the grasslands they call home.

Camera traps snap photos when zebras walk by. Scientists use stripes to track each zebra.

GLOSSARY

foal
A baby zebra.

poaching
Hunting animals when
it is against the law.

bachelor
A male Zebra that has
not yet found a herd of
his own

savanna
A wide, flat grassland
with few trees where
many animals live

Serengeti
A vast grassland in
Tanzania, Africa, where
huge herds of zebras
and other animals live
and migrate.

9 798898 181161